The Love
Coloring Book

Adult Colouring Books

Aryla Publishing 2020

978-1-912675-63-0

www.arylapublishing.com

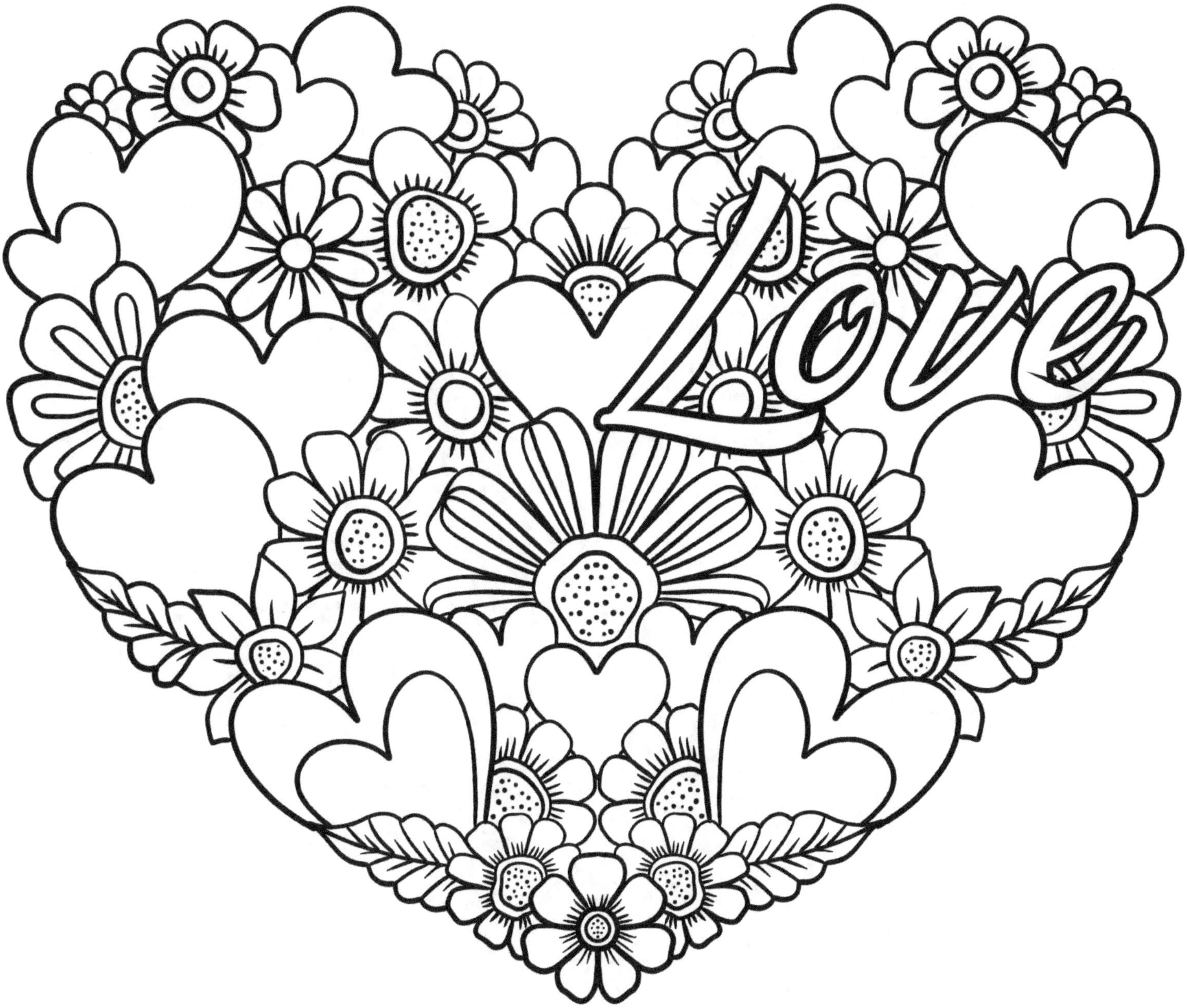
Love

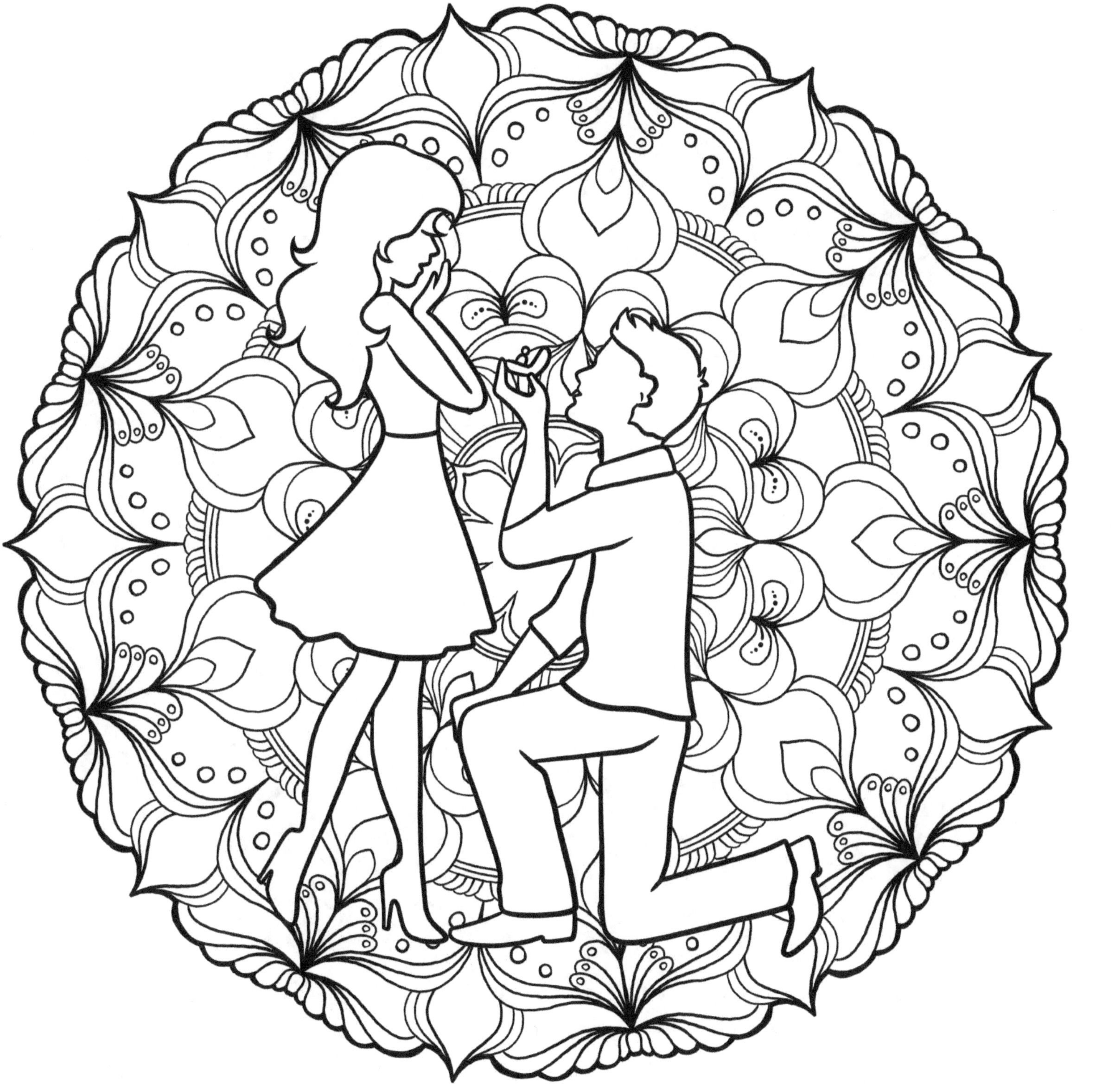

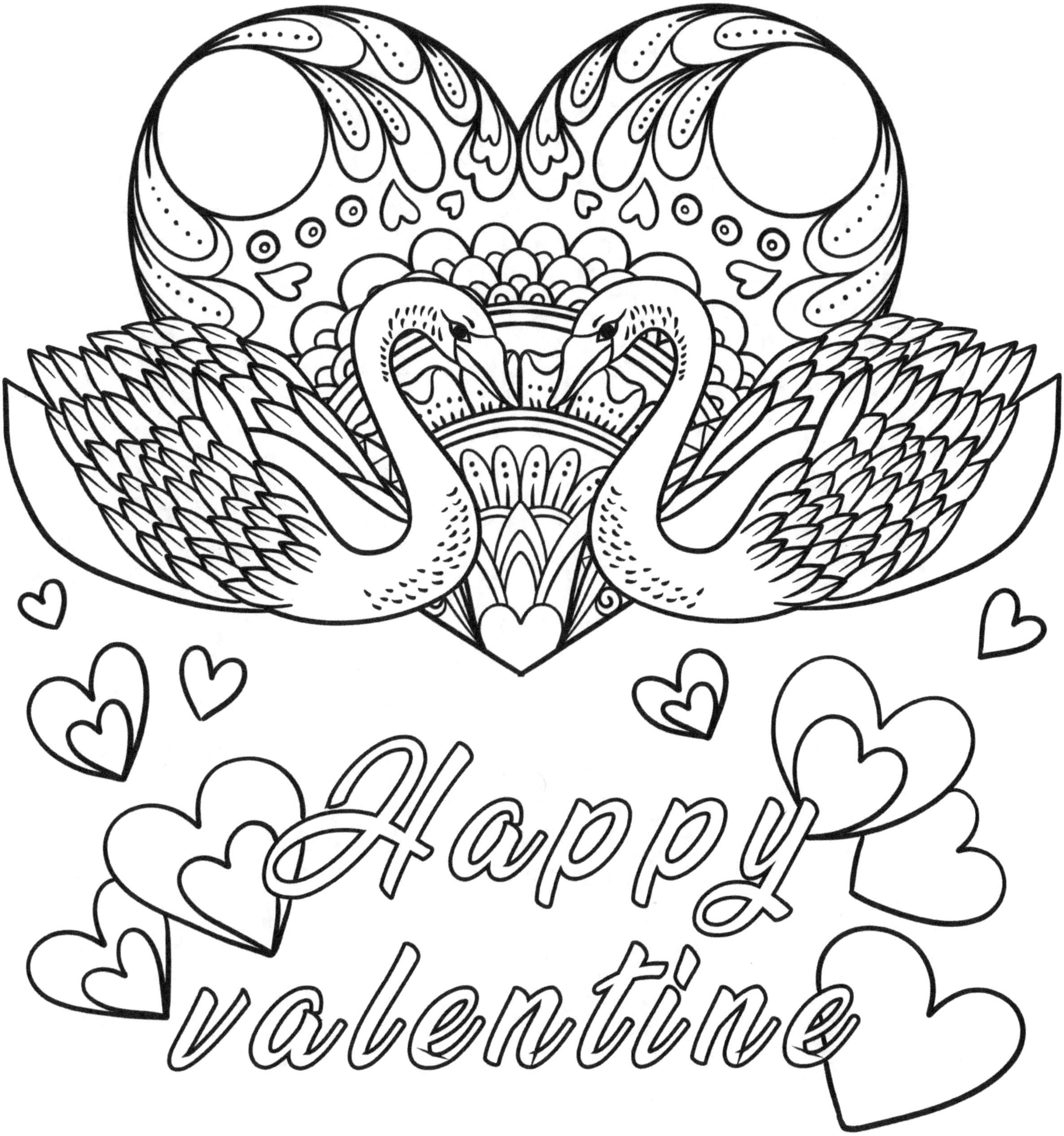
Happy
valentine

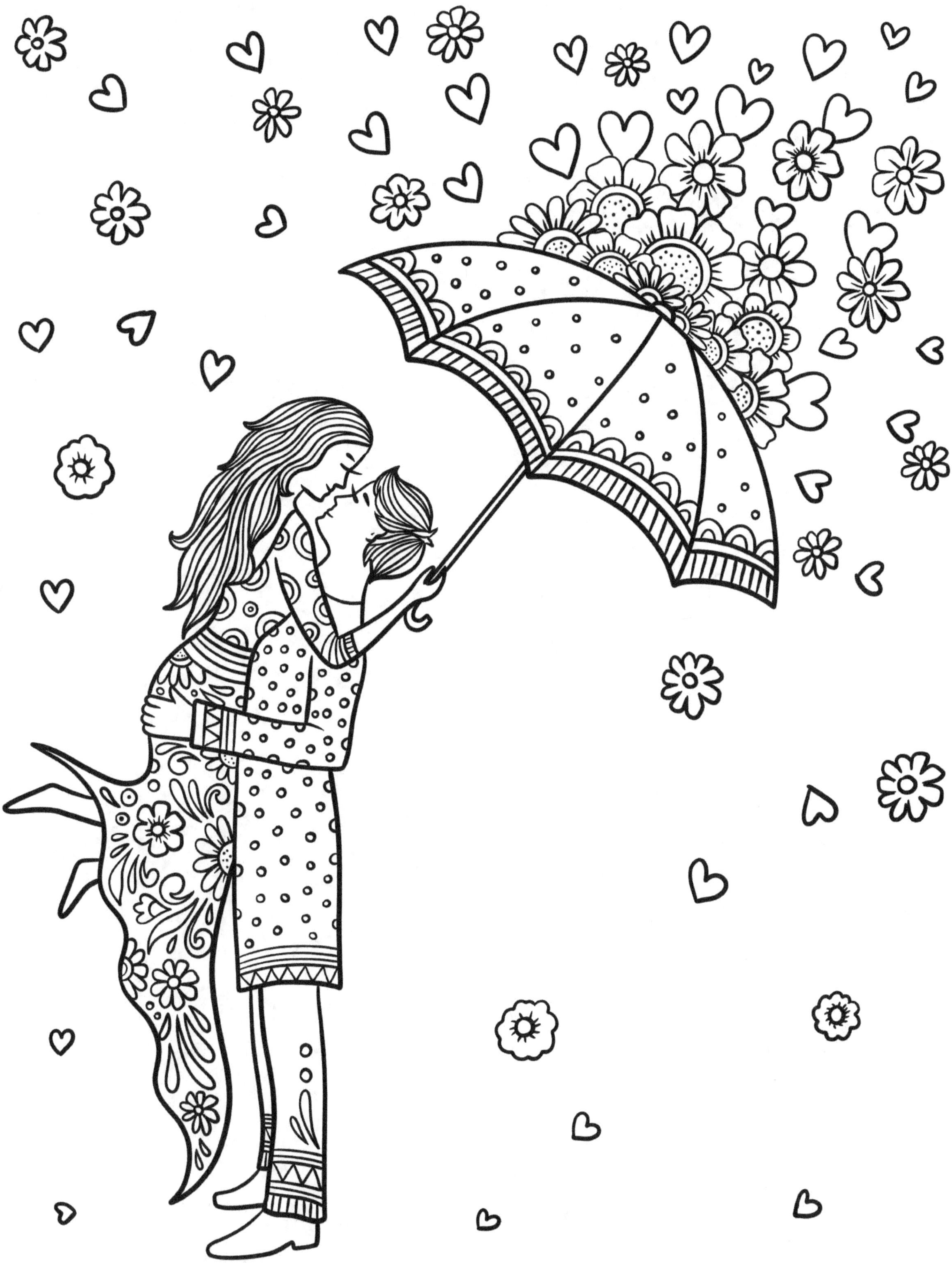

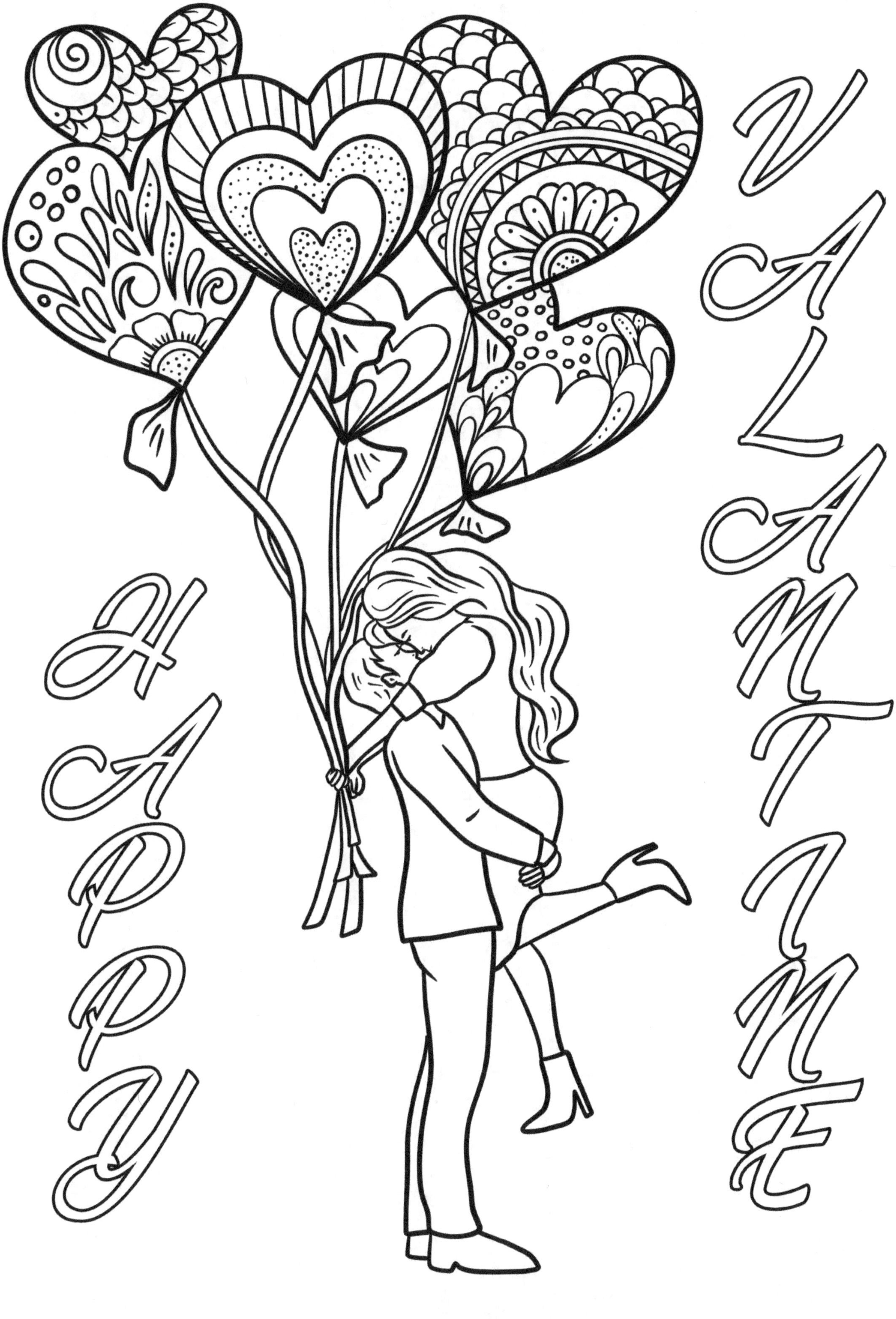
HAPPY
VALENTINE

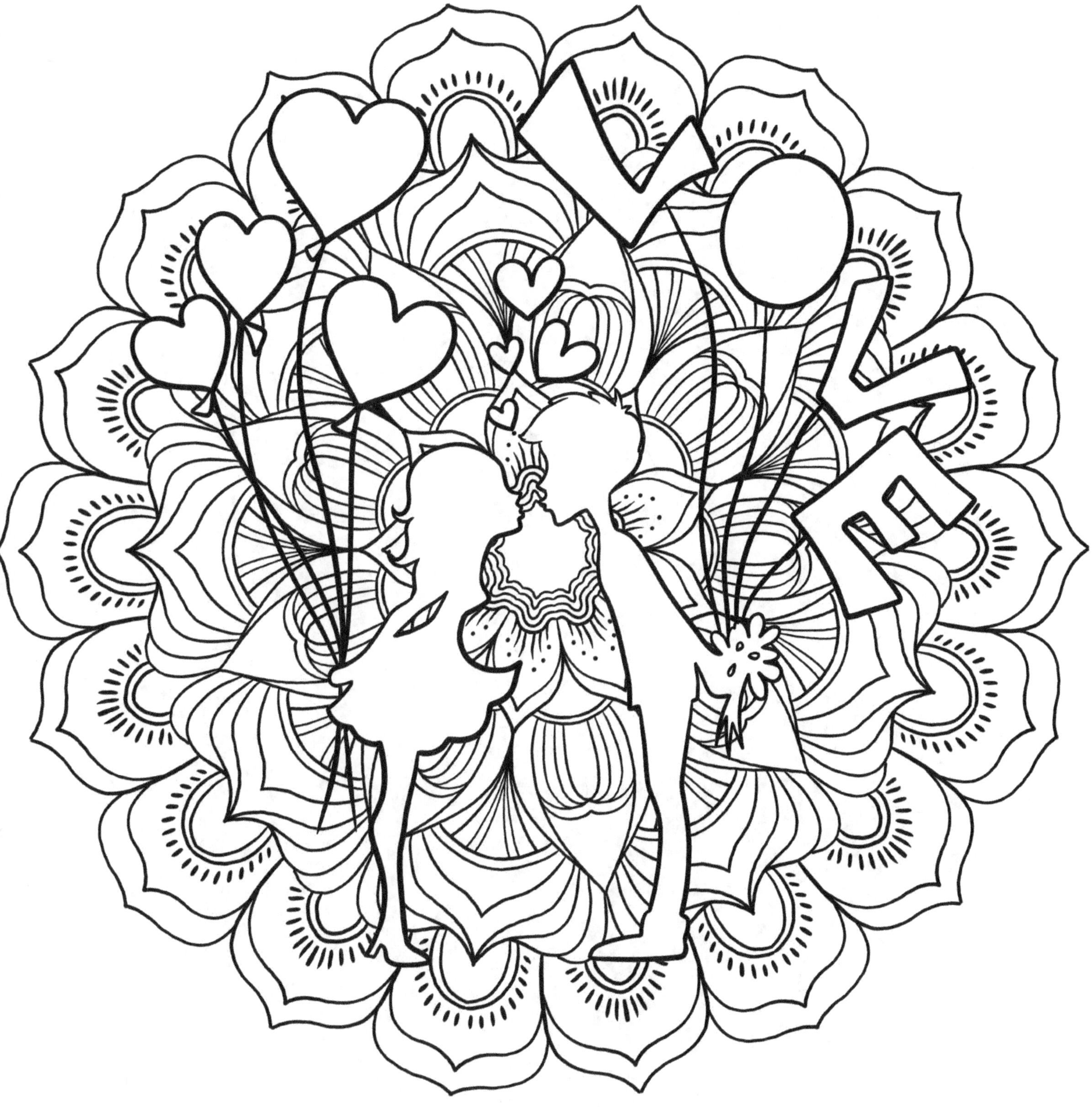
LOVE

I LOVE YOU

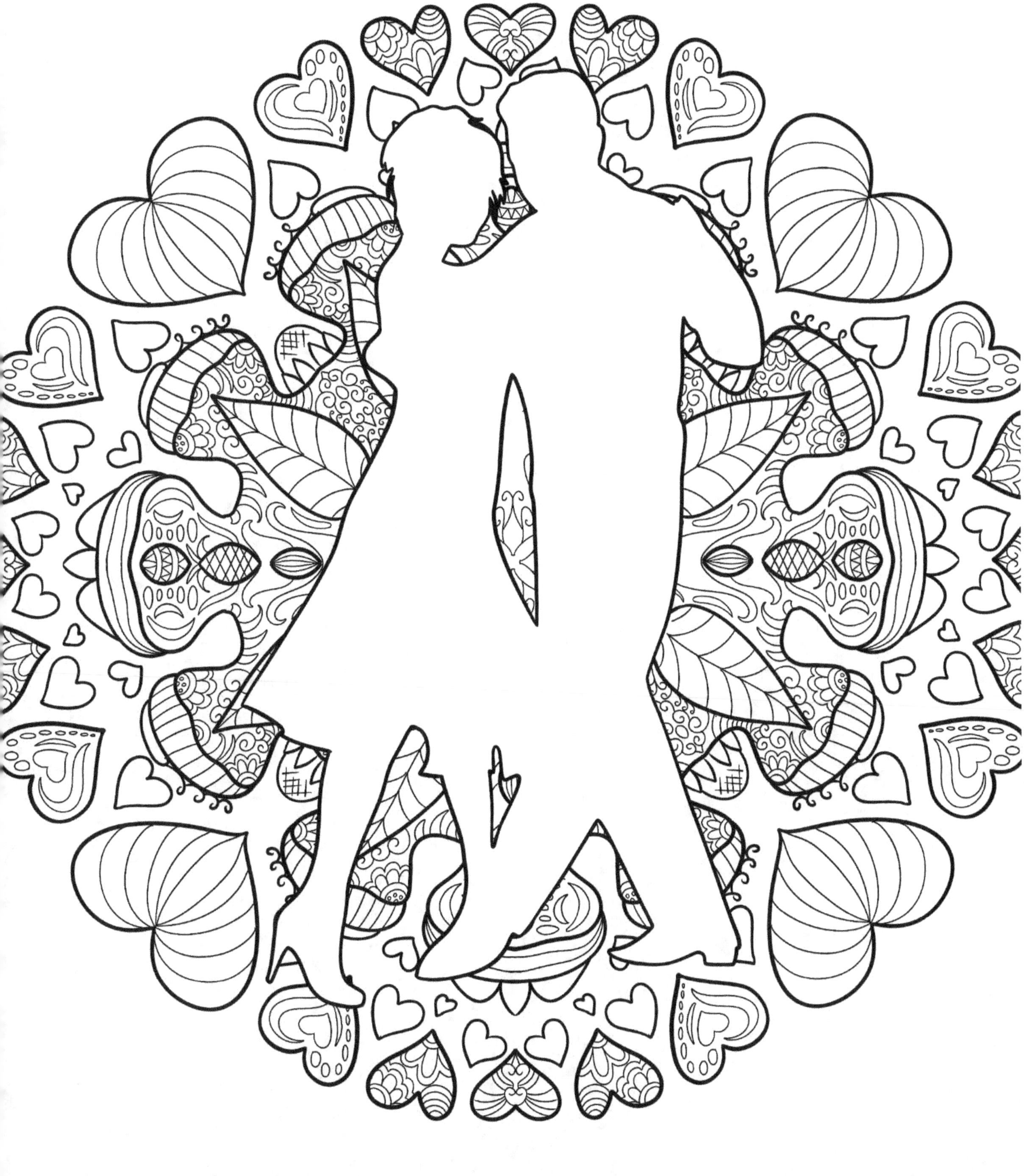

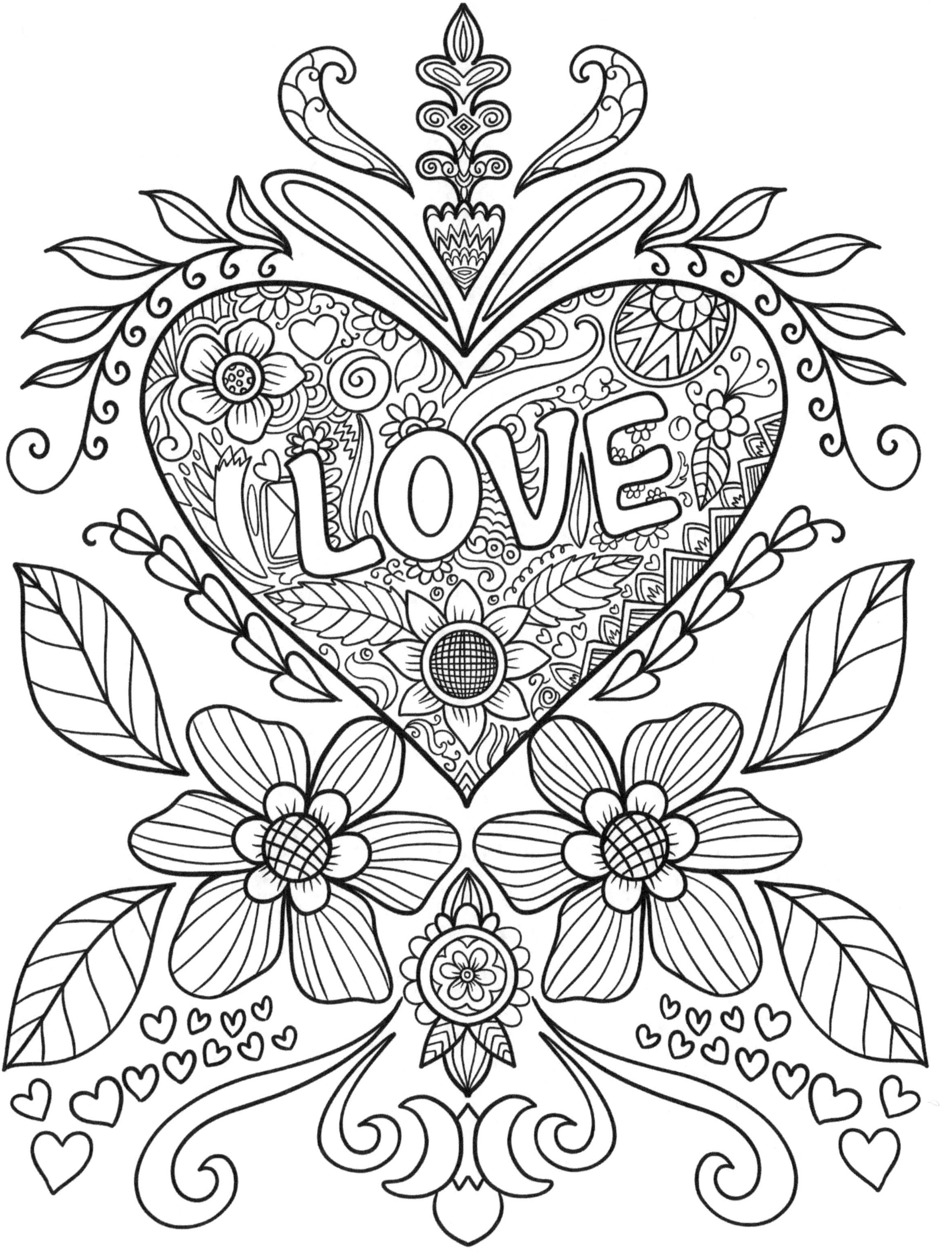
LOVE

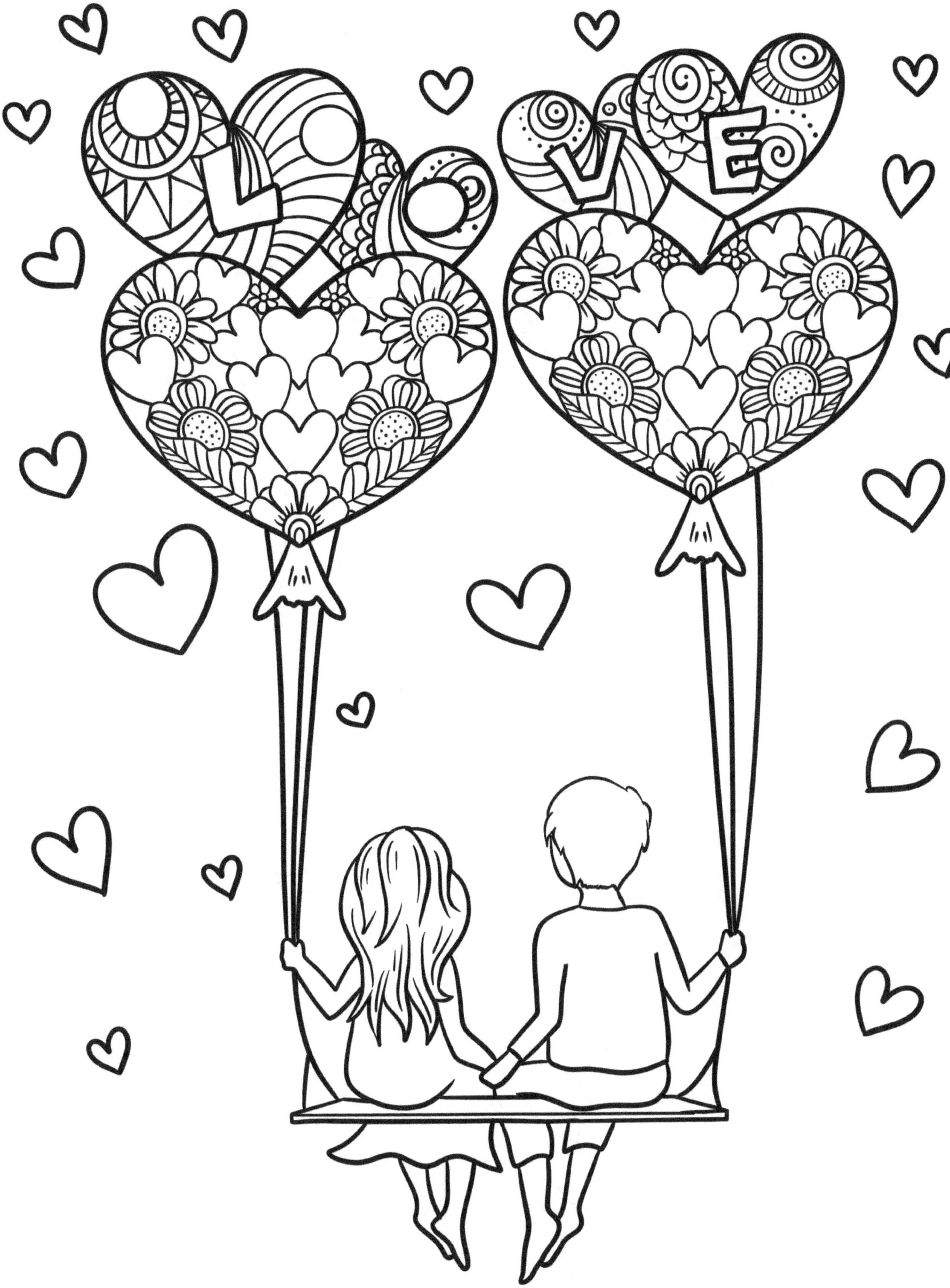
L
O
V
E

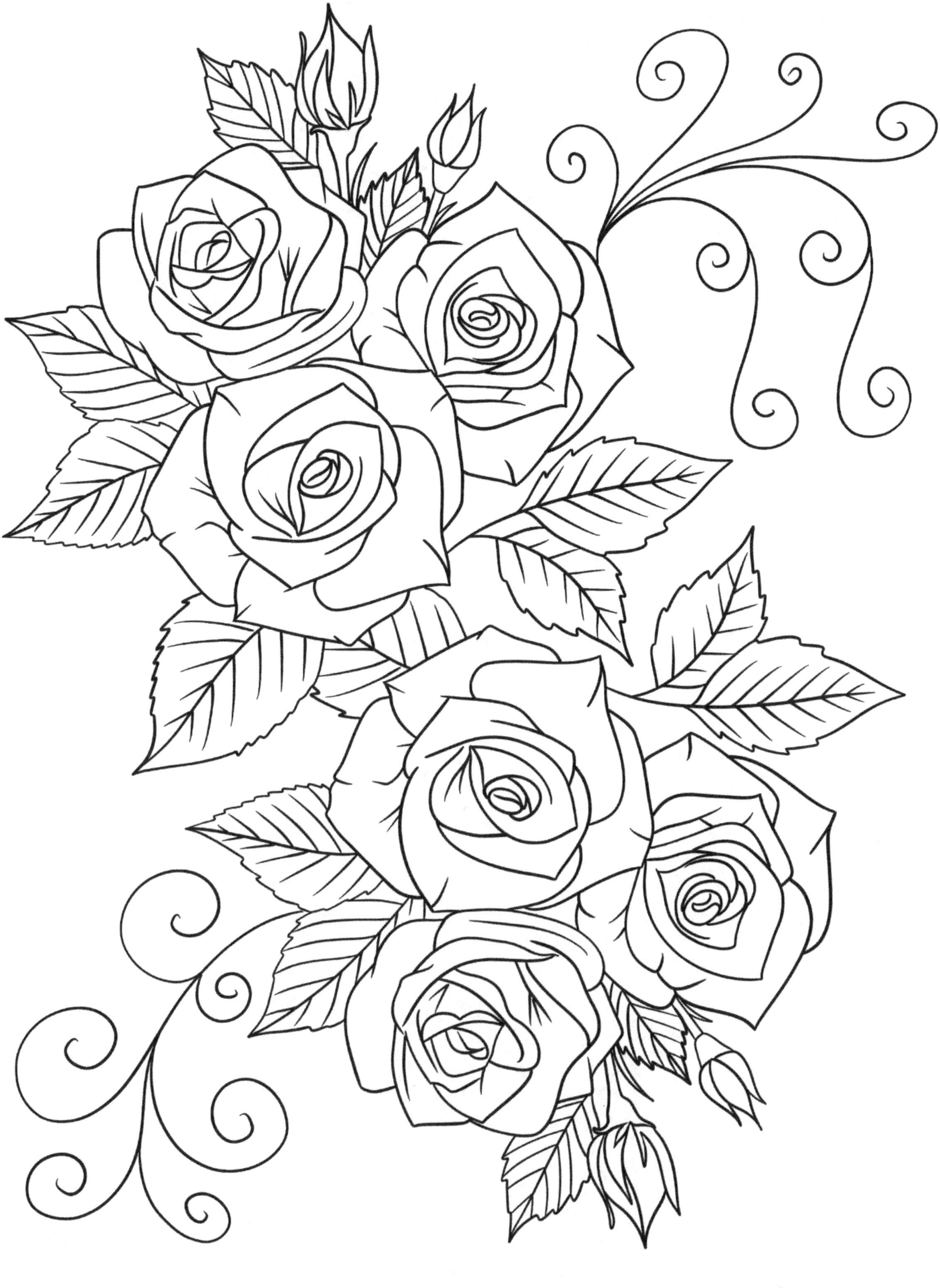

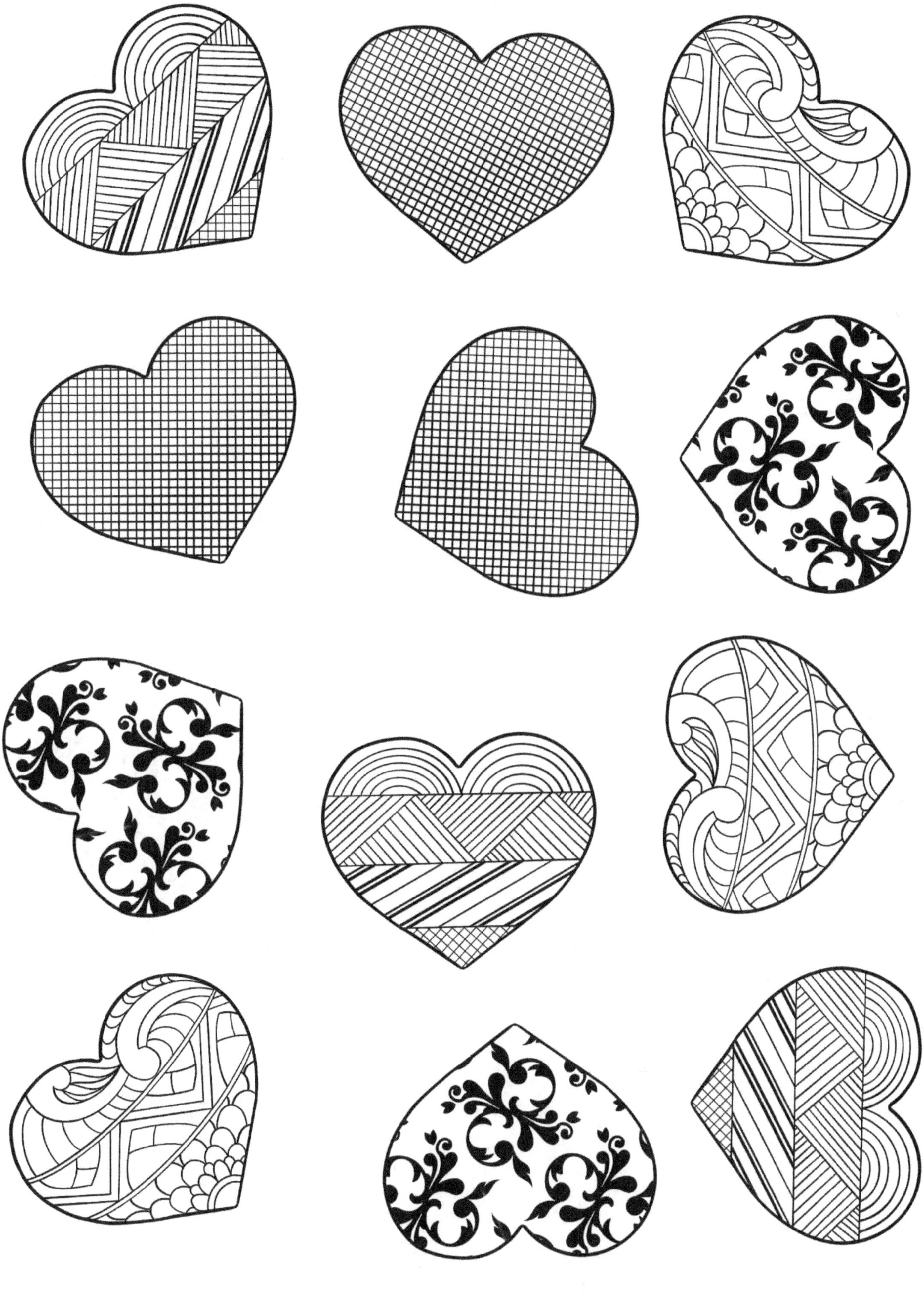

LOVE YOU

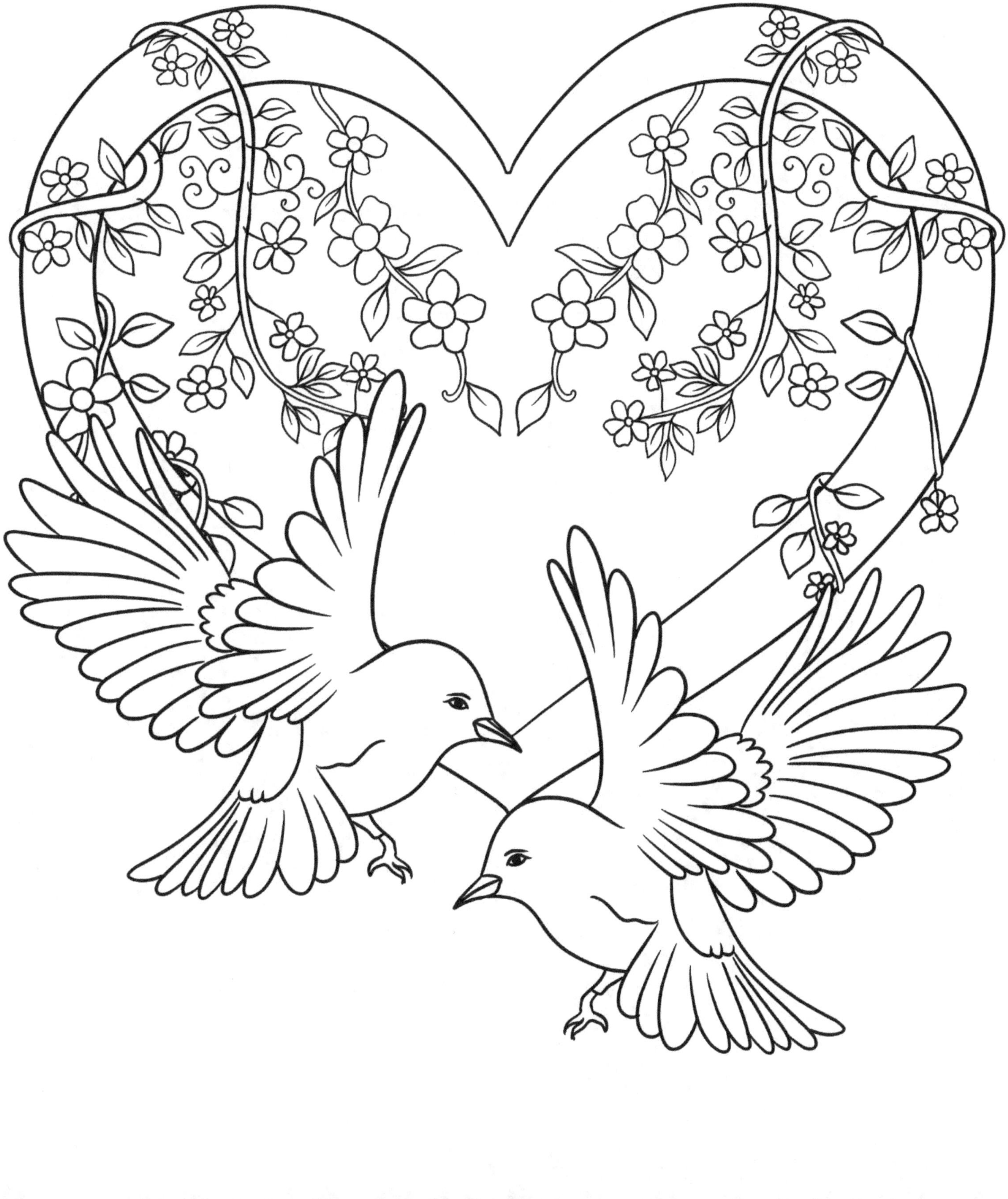

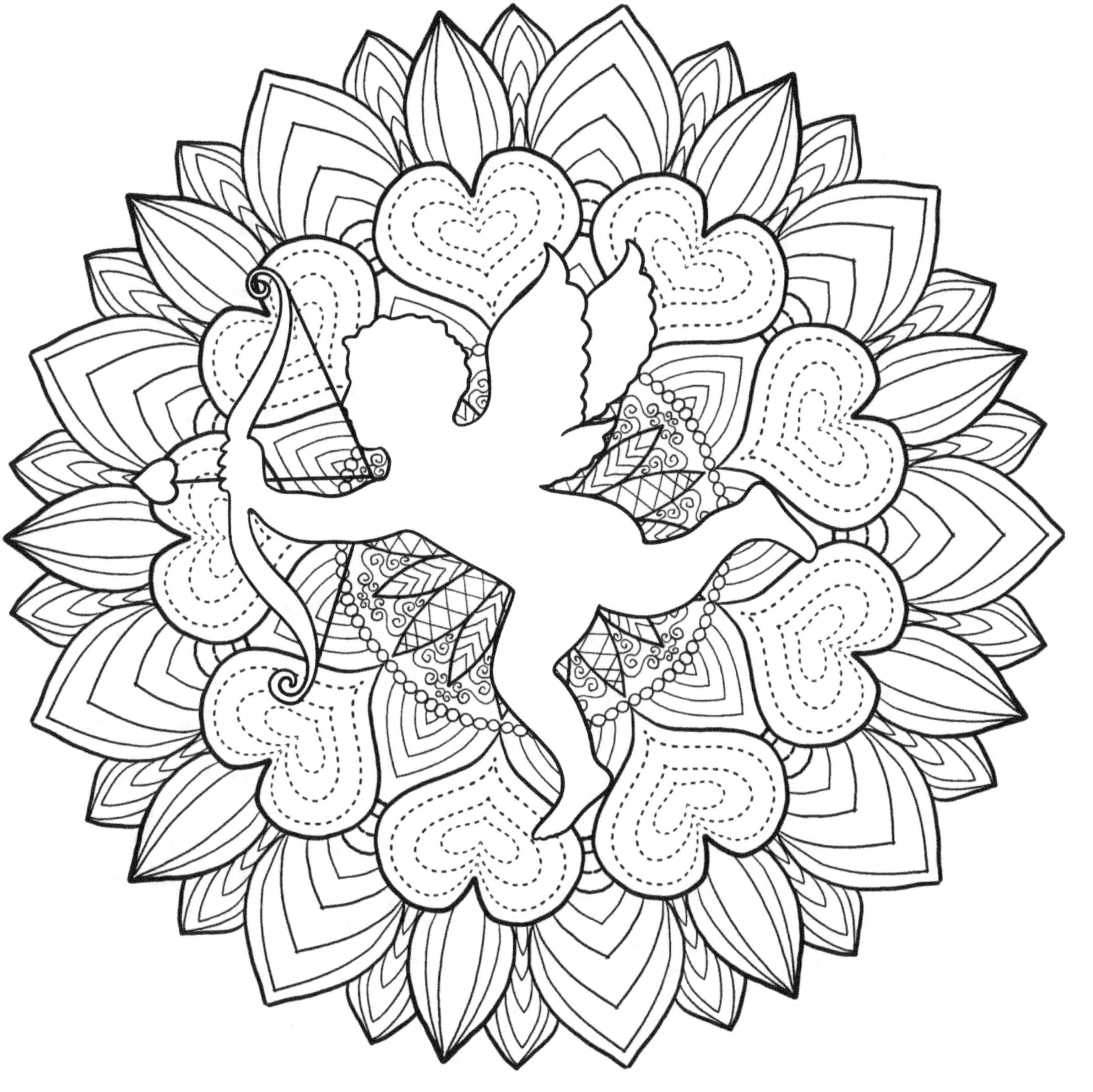

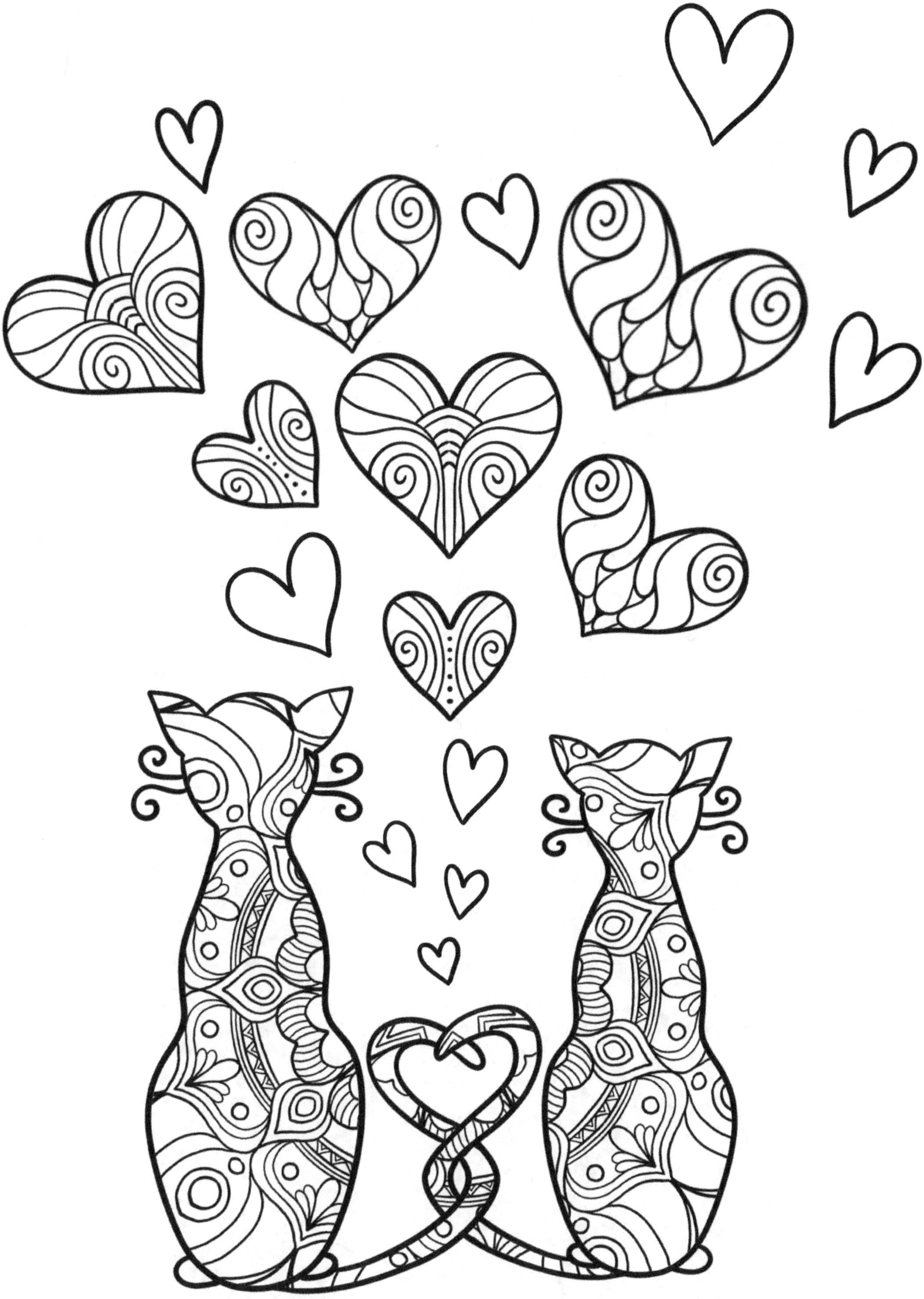

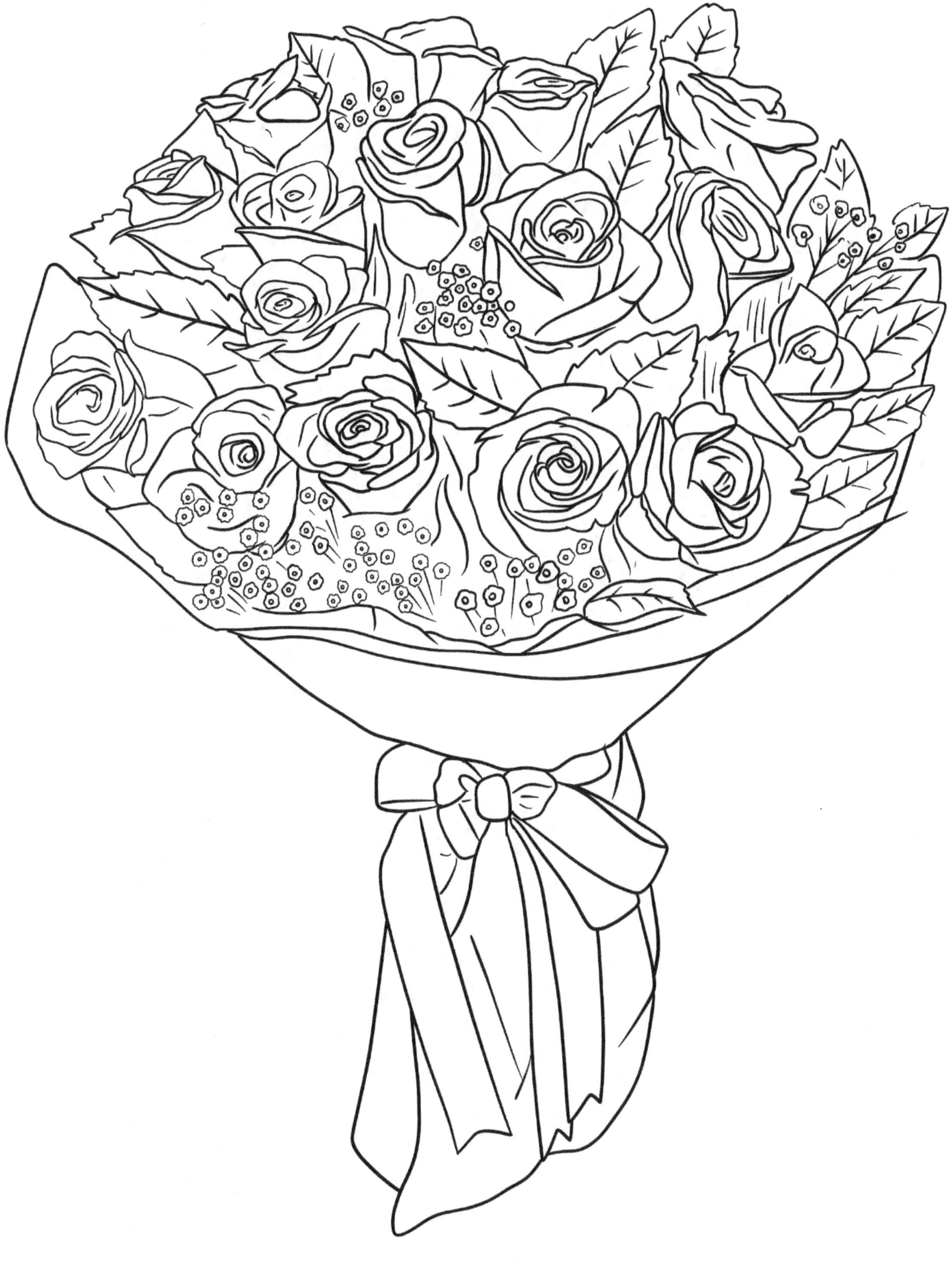

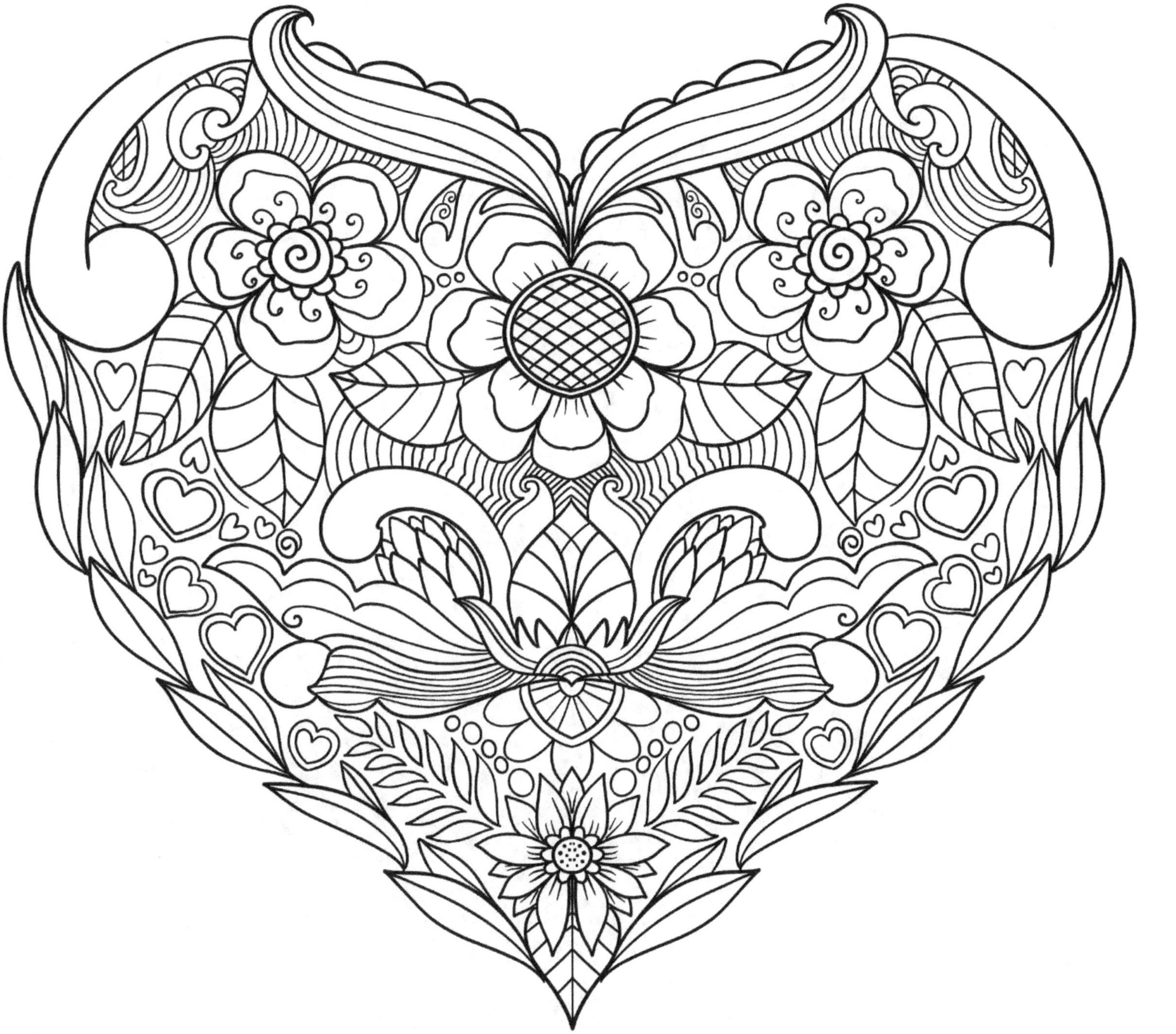

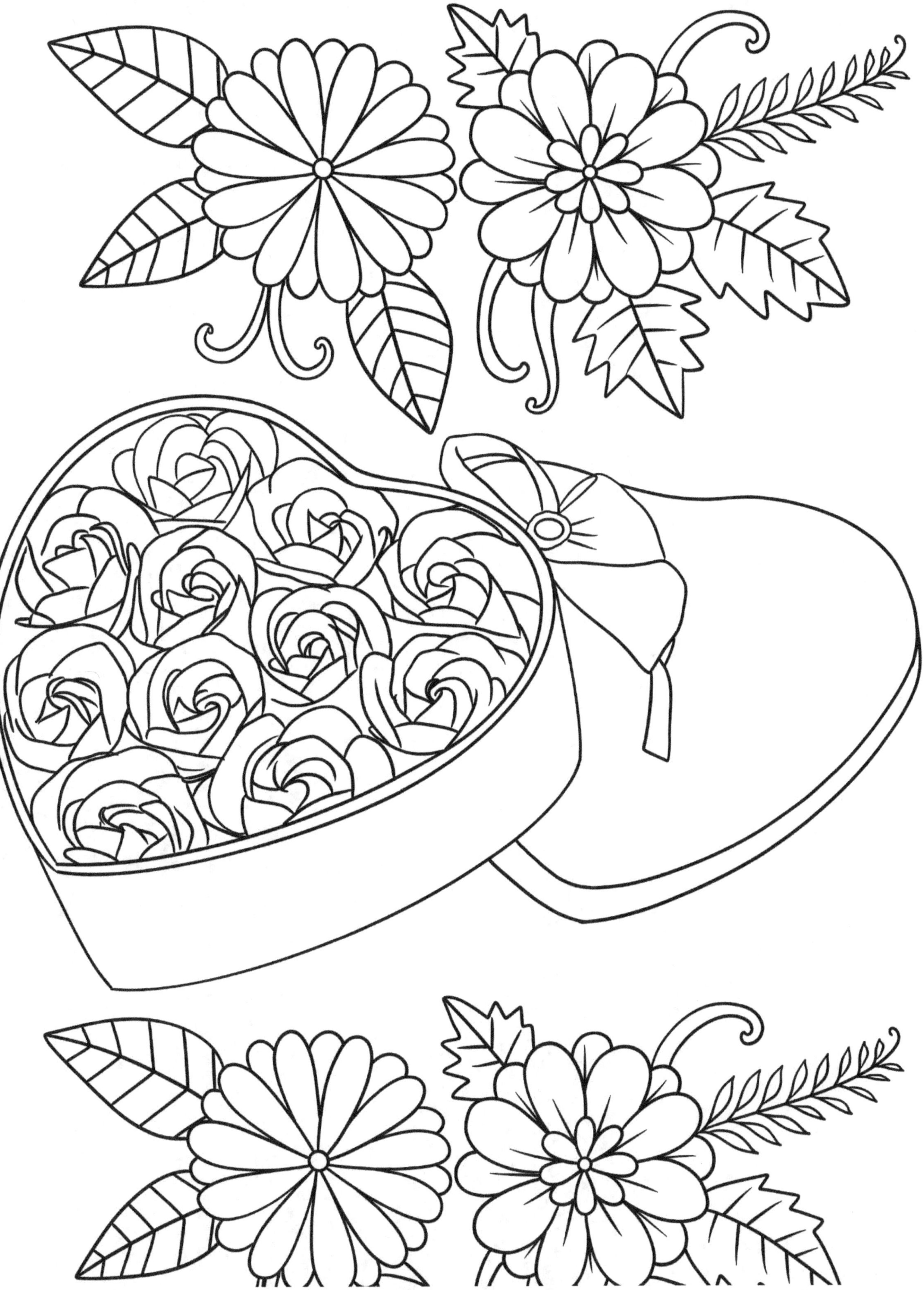

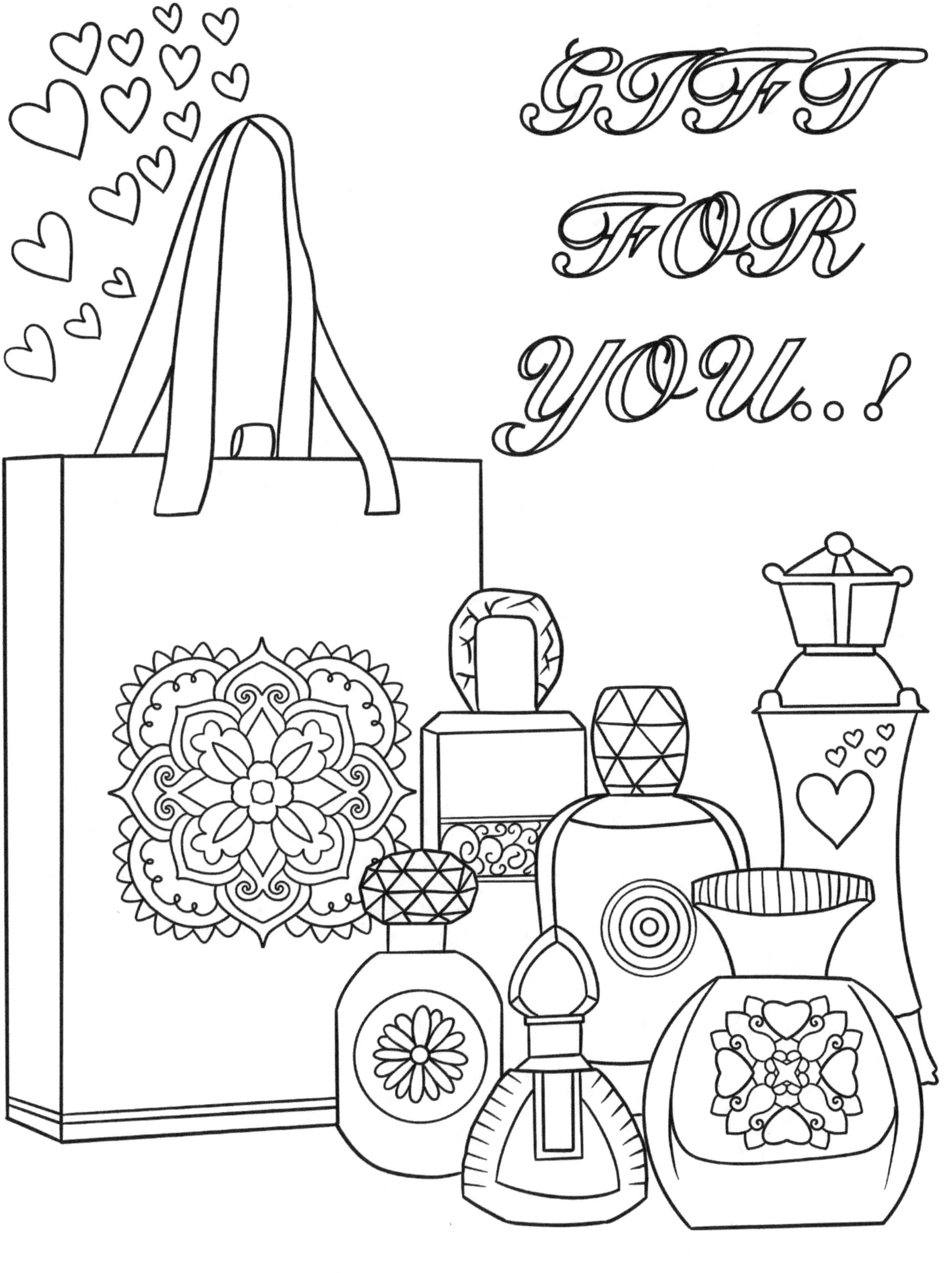
GIFT
FOR
YOU..!

LOVE
LOVE
LOVE
LOVE

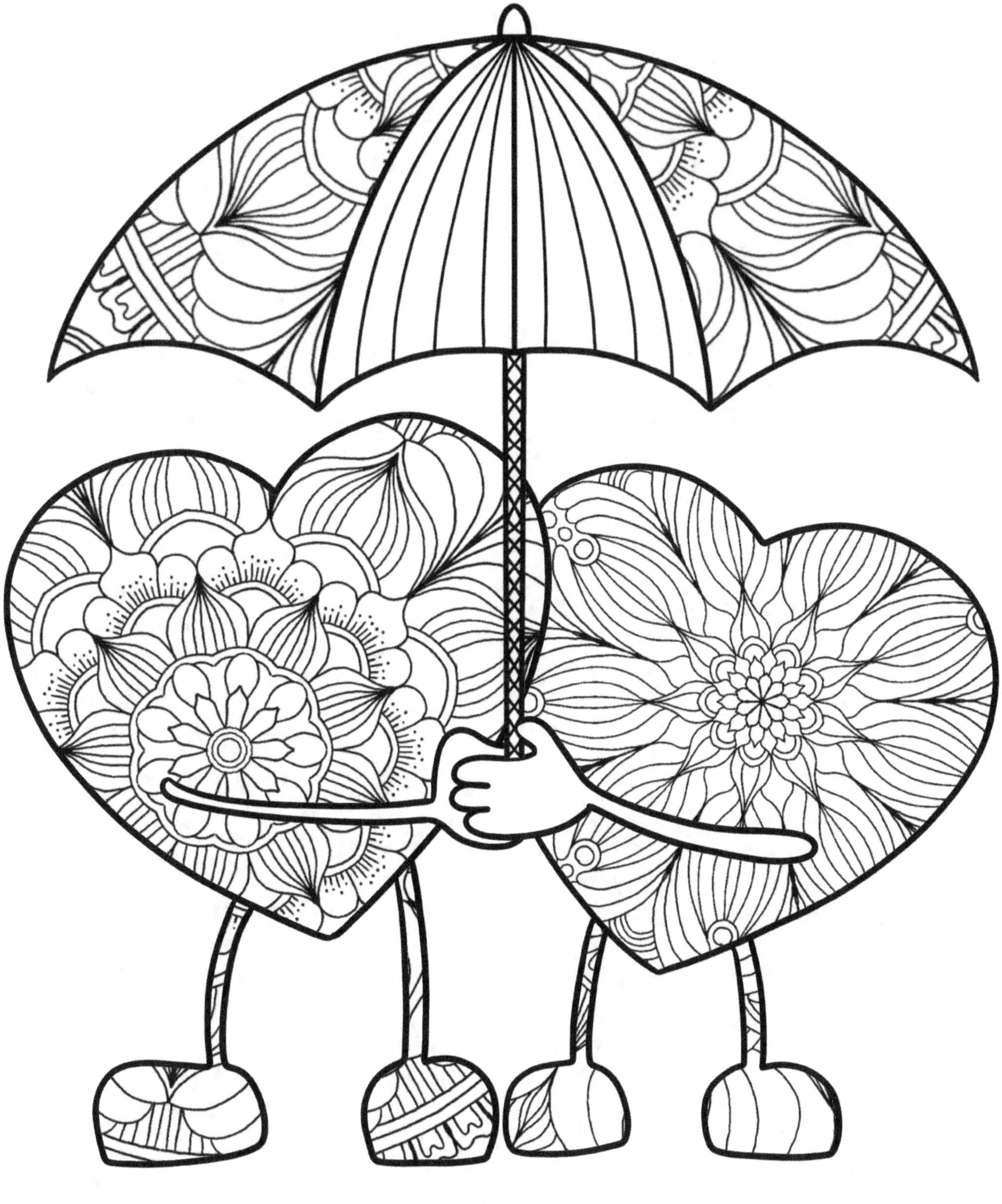

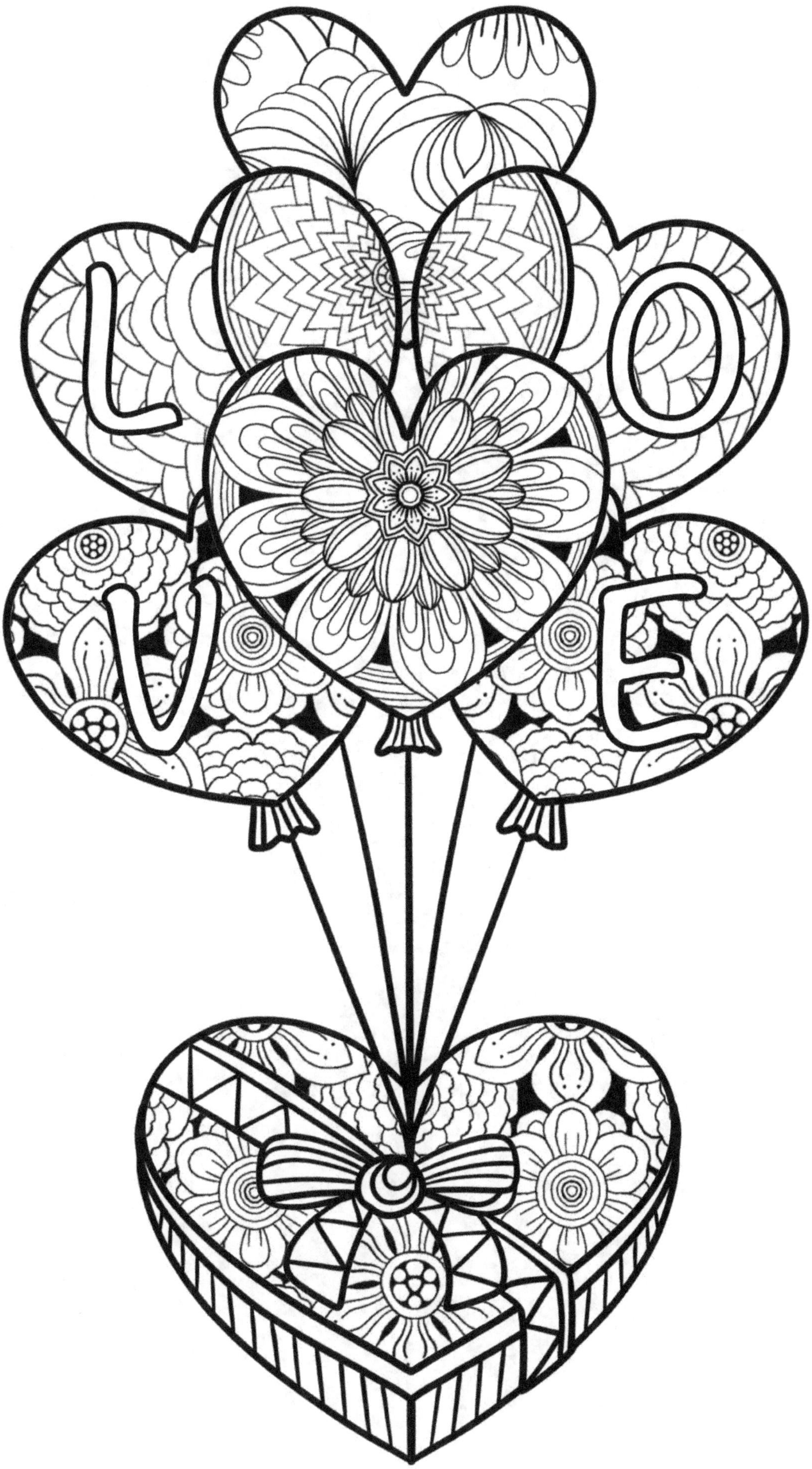
L O V E

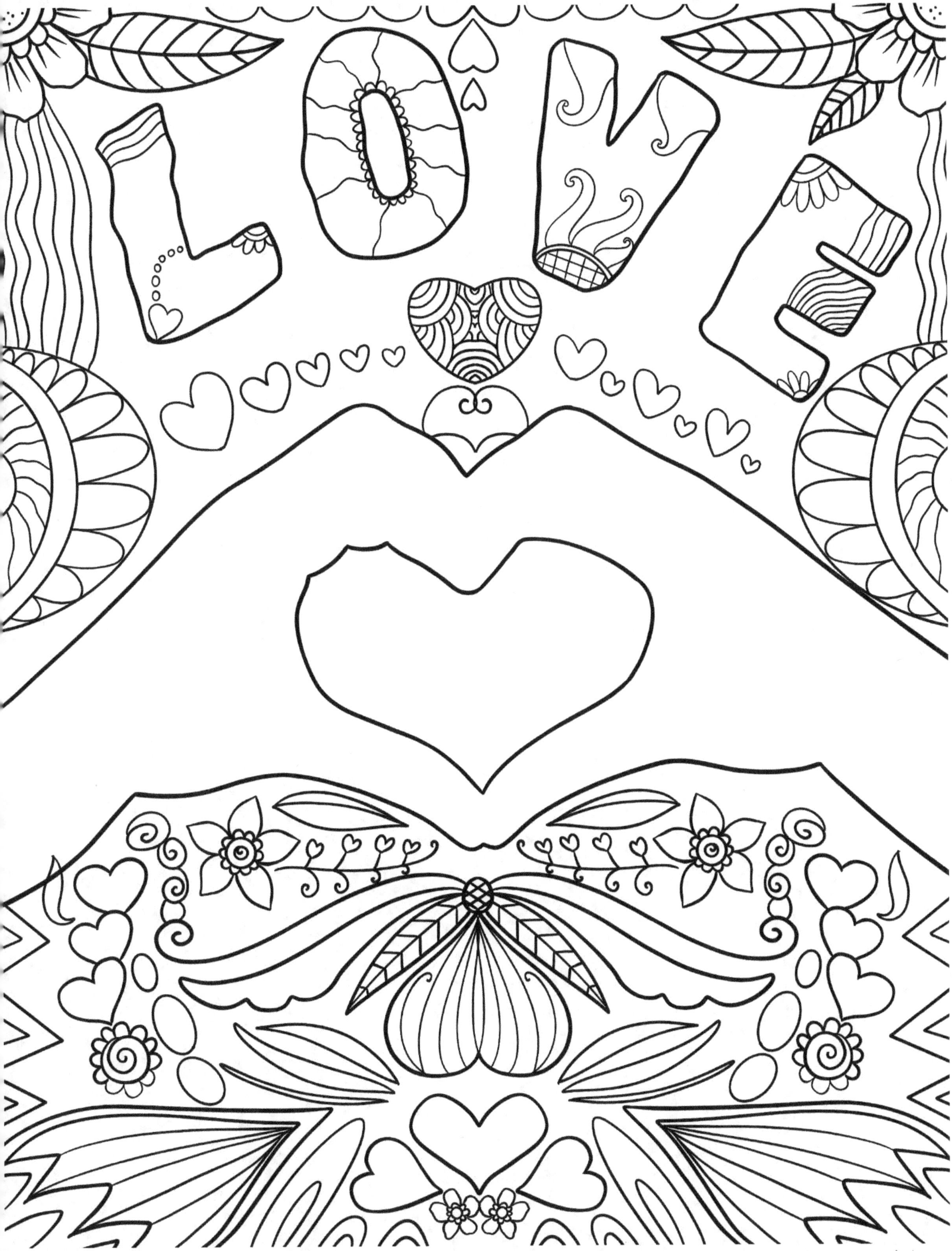
LOVE

Thank you for purchasing this book.

If you would like to know more about Aryla Publishing Books please visit:-

www.ArylaPublishing.com

Or follow us on
Facebook
Twitter
Instagram
for *free promotions*

@arylapublishing

We would love to know what you think of this book so please leave us a review.

Have a wonderful day ☺

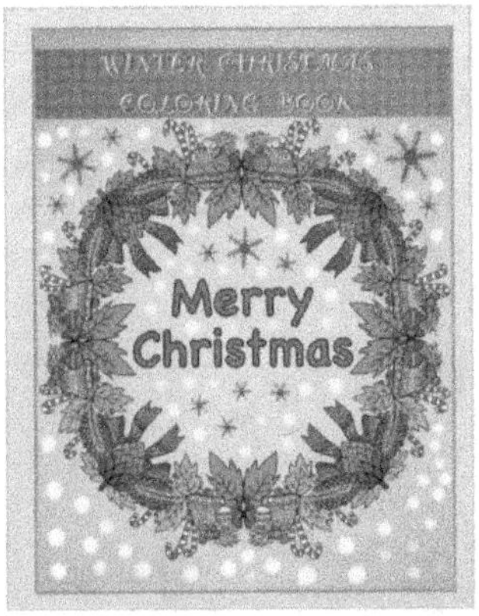
Merry Christmas

UNDER THE SEA
COLORING BOOK

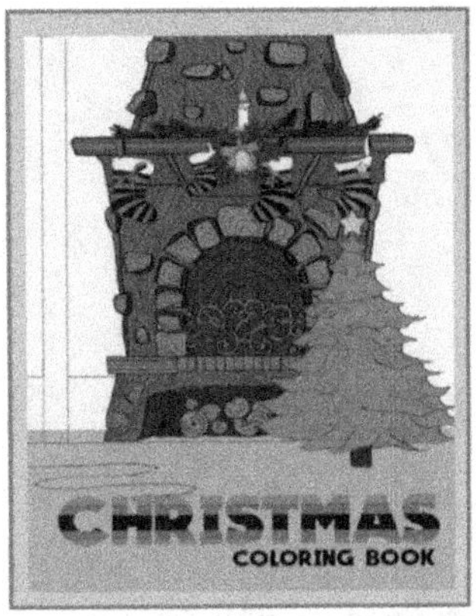
CHRISTMAS
COLORING BOOK

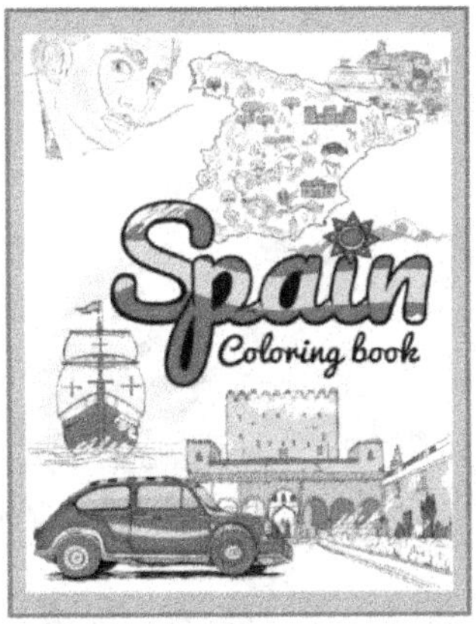
Spain
Coloring book

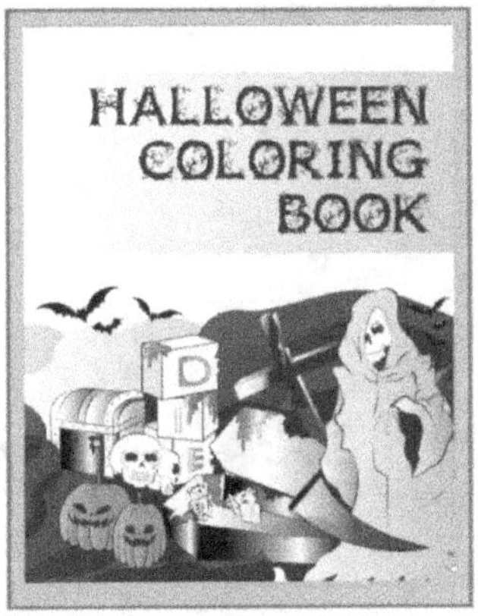
HALLOWEEN
COLORING
BOOK

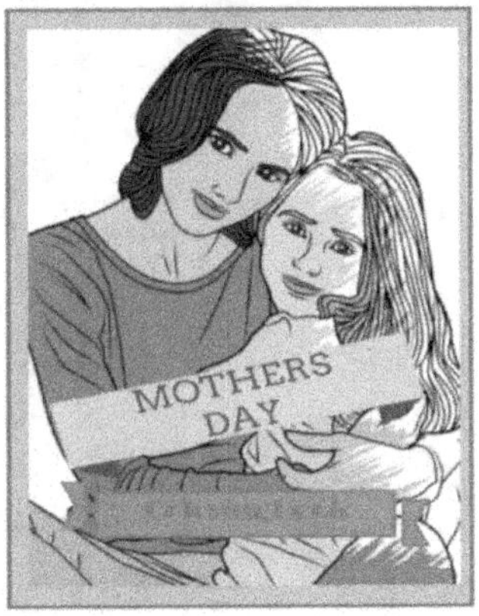
MOTHERS
DAY

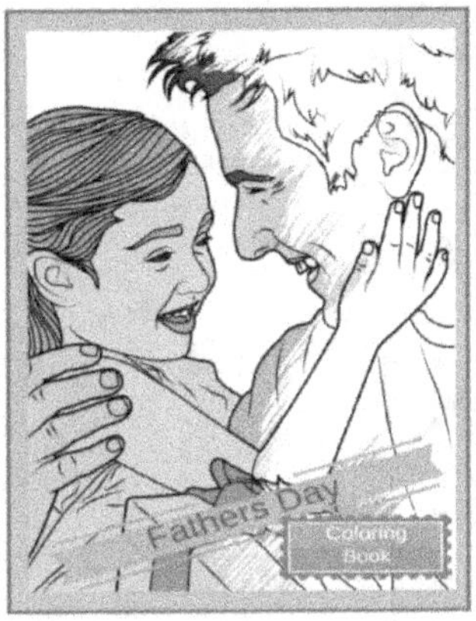
Fathers Day
Coloring
Book

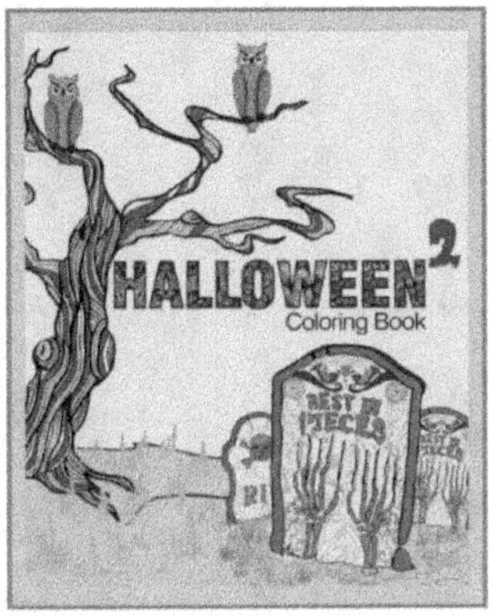
HALLOWEEN 2
Coloring Book

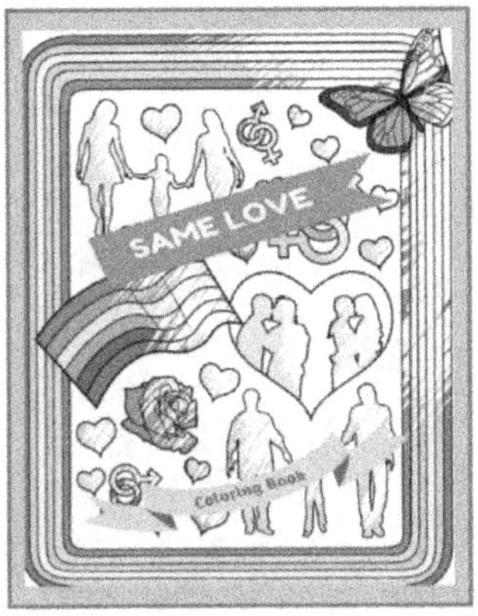
SAME LOVE
Coloring Book

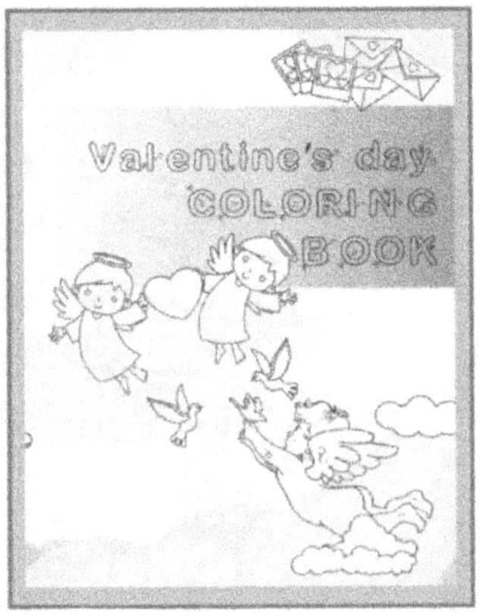
Valentine's day
COLORING
BOOK

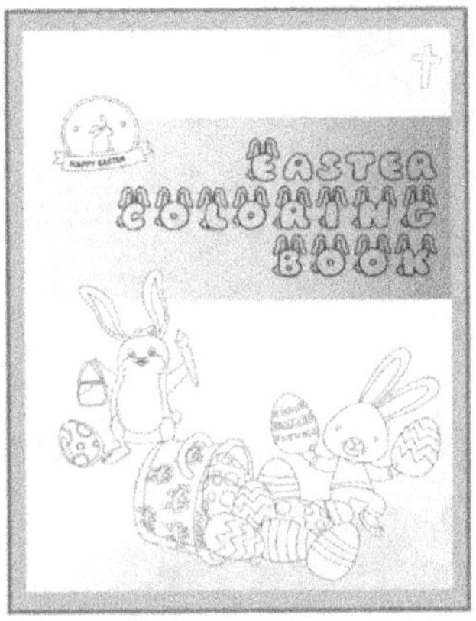
EASTER
COLORING
BOOK

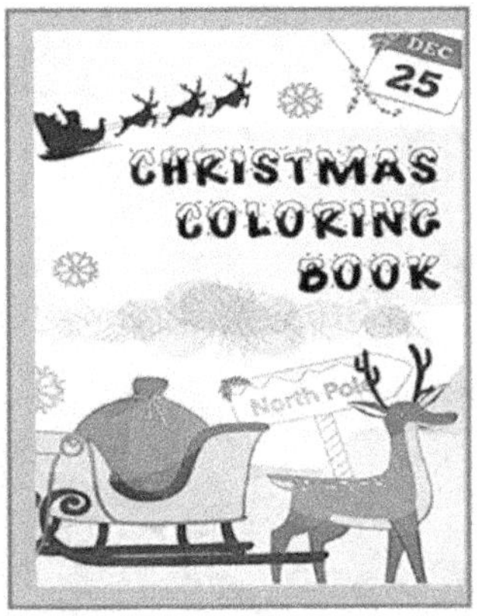
DEC
25
CHRISTMAS
COLORING
BOOK

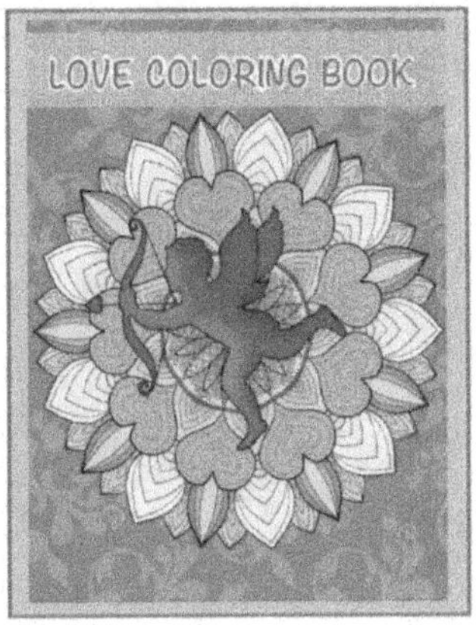
LOVE COLORING BOOK

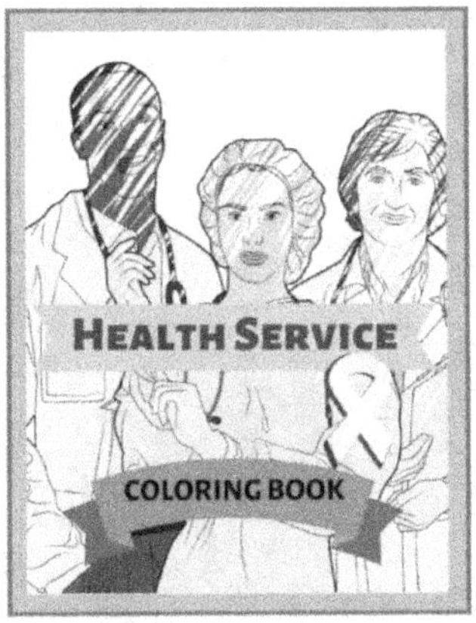
HEALTH SERVICE
COLORING BOOK

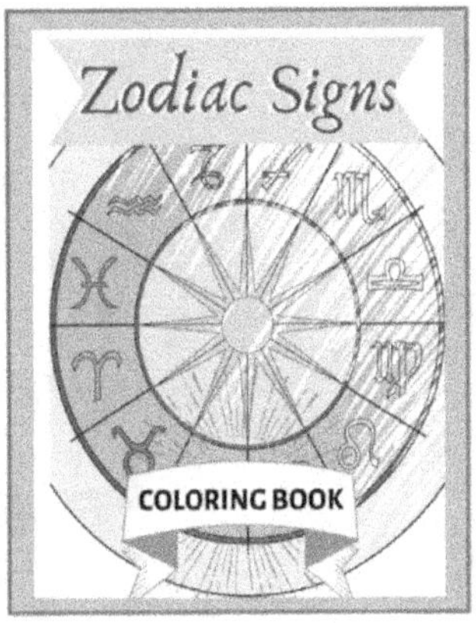
Zodiac Signs
COLORING BOOK

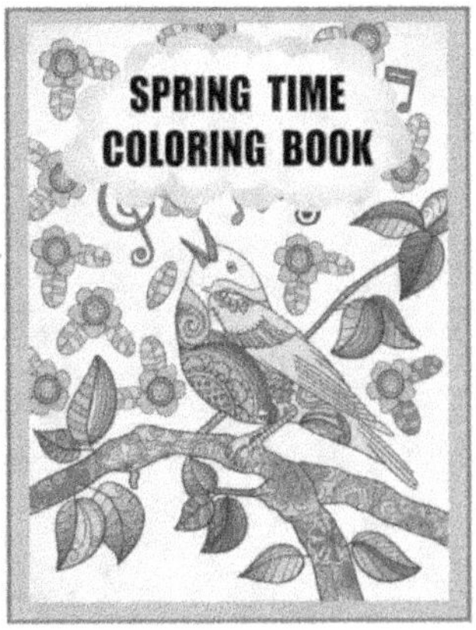
SPRING TIME
COLORING BOOK

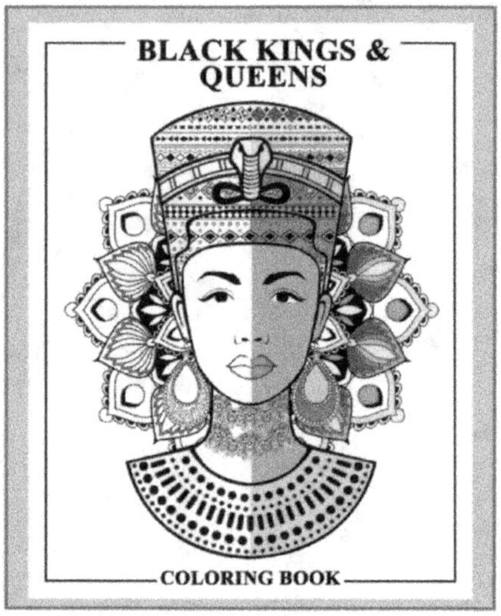
BLACK KINGS &
QUEENS
COLORING BOOK

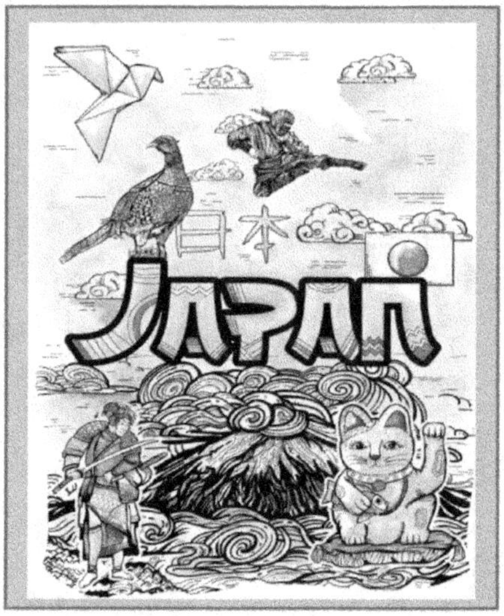
日本
JAPAN

Color In Fun
Kids Books

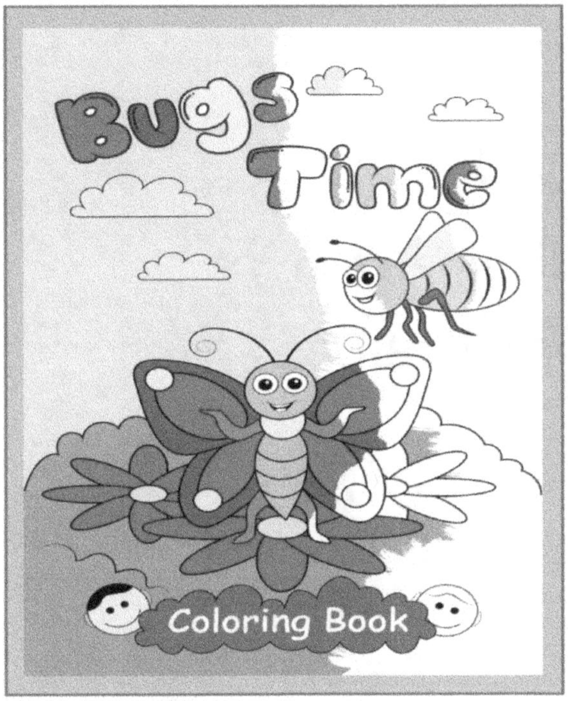

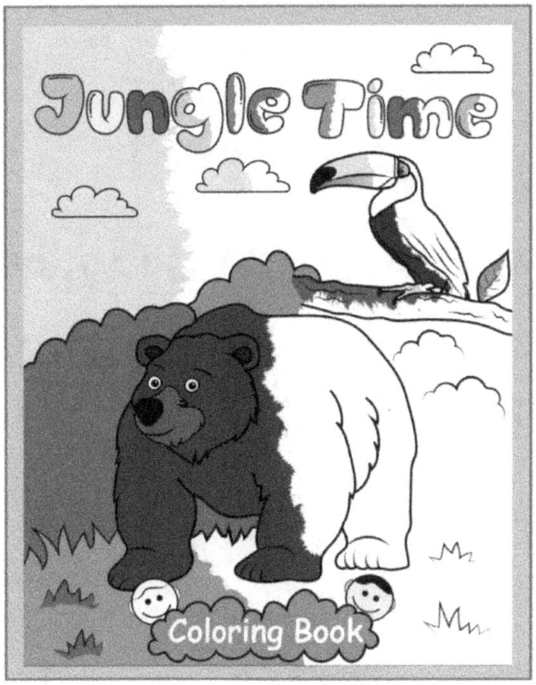

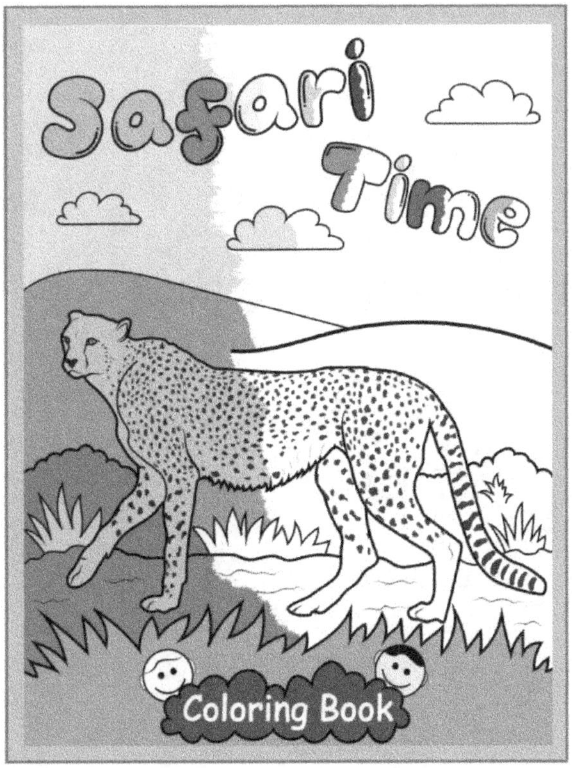

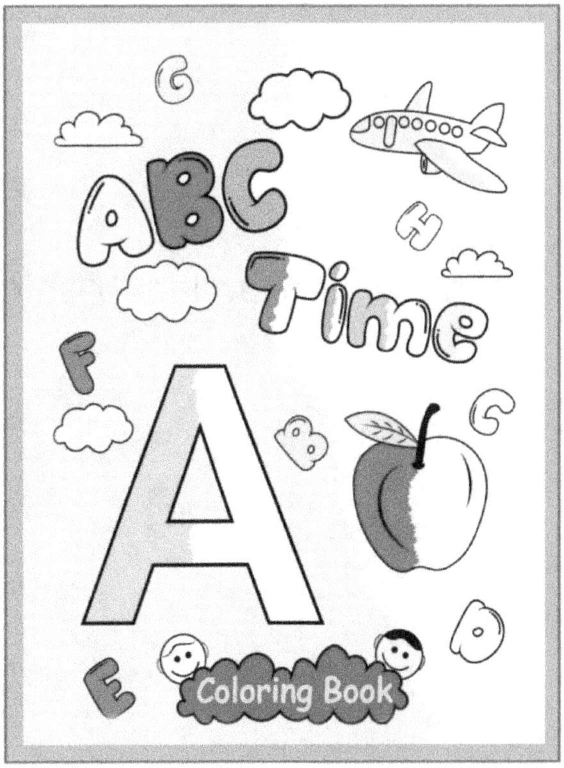

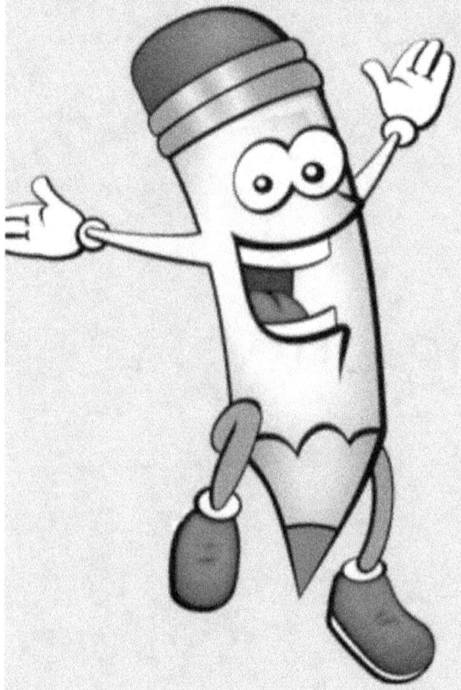

WE WOULD LOVE YOUR FEEDBACK

PLEASE LEAVE REVIEW AT:-

https://bit.ly/Lovecoloringbook